My Horse Samson

BY
ASHLEY BALL

Ashley Ball

Headline Kids
an imprint of Headline Books, Inc.
Terra Alta, WV

My Horse
Samson

by Ashley Ball

Cover photo by Connor Photography

To order additional copies of this book
or for book publishing information, or to contact the author:

Headline Kids
P. O. Box 52
Terra Alta, WV 26764
www.headlinekids.com

Tel: 800-570-5951
Email: mybook@headlinebooks.com
www.headlinebooks.com

Published by Headline Books

ISBN-13: 978-0-938467-10-6

Library of Congress Cataloging-in-Publication Data

Ball, Ashley.
My horse Samson / by Ashley Ball.
    p. cm.
ISBN 978-0-938467-10-6
1. Horse adoption--Juvenile literature. 2. Animal rescue--Juvenile literature.
3. Show jumping--Juvenile literature. I. Title.
SF302.B353 2011
636.1--dc22
                            2011005781

PRINTED IN THE UNITED STATES OF AMERICA

To Mom and Dad.

Preface

I can feel their eyes on me as I lead Samson into the State Fair ring.

I try to ignore them and guide Samson to each jump, letting him sniff and look over each jump barrier. He's just four years old and nervous—this is something I always let him do to show him the jumps won't hurt him.

Samson has never seen so many people before or such bright lights at night, or heard the loud screaming music of the band, Hinder, playing on stage behind the arena. I've shown horses before, earning hundreds of ribbons over the past five years; I can shut it all out. And Samson can too, once I get him to settle down and listen to me. But, right now he's spooking and bulging, moving his rear toward the inside of the ring as he looks at all the people moving in the stands. What a commotion! And, the people are looking back at me, like I shouldn't have brought such a young skittish horse to the State competition.

I remembered the "horse whisperer" from Hawaii saying, "Breathe slowly and opposite the horse to calm, and settle. When he breathes out, you breathe in; and when he breathes in, you breathe out! You let him know that you are calm and relaxed."

Samson and I walk slowly back to the starting line just outside the ring and wait in position. I breathe slowly and opposite Samson. We wait.

Finally, it's our turn to compete. I kick Samson into a canter and we take the jumps—including a 3-foot-6-inch OXER (two jumps with two rails) and the crowd's jaws drop.

They're looking at us in a different way now!

The judges announce the results. Samson and I are tied for GRAND CHAMPION with Destiny, a girl I know from 4-H camp, and her nine-year-old Thoroughbred horse, Steel.

Can you believe it? Of all the horses and riders in this State competition, Destiny, and I are tied for first! If there is anyone, other than me, who I would want to be Grand Champion, it would be my good friend and 4-H pal, Destiny. Now, we are facing each other in a two-team run-off on a course neither of us expected!

Placing so high is pretty remarkable for a four-year-old horse that was almost thrown away!

Chapter 1:
Four Years Ago

I begged my parents for a horse since I was small. One day we read in the newspaper about some horses from around Birds Creek, WV—a small community in my county—that were abused, neglected, starved, and forced to breed. Looking at the black and white photographs, I could even make out their bones. They had been left to die! Mom looked at me and said, "We can go look at them and see how they are doing now if you would like." I was so excited, but I was also prepared to see the worst. Next day after school, I hopped in the truck and we soon approached the Rescue Farm on a winding dirt road. Huge pastures were on each side of the road. Before the truck even stopped, I opened the door and the scent of horses and grass filled my nose. It gave me a warm, fuzzy feeling.

The barn keeper approached us dressed in her old, worn-out jeans and plaid shirt. She said just two words to us, "Come on!" I scurried behind the tall blonde woman. Then she whistled very loudly. A huge herd of

Samson with his mother

horses ran down the hill and to the gate where we were standing. One in particular stood out to me, a medium-sized white horse with brown on the sides of her face. She was beautiful! As I looked over the rest of the horses, I overheard Mom and the woman talking. The woman was saying, "We have them all fat and healthy now. They are ready for adoption today. The black and white mare over there is pregnant. We are not sure how much longer she has until she has her baby, because the only stallion died of starvation some time ago."

My mom seemed interested in the black and white mare. But I sure did love that white mare. Mom walked over to me and asked, "So, which one do you like?" Excitedly, I showed her the white mare. She said she liked the pregnant black mare, too.

The tall young woman said, "Well, you would probably be better with two so they don't get too stressed from being alone."

Mom asked, "How much for the two mares to be adopted?"

Mom and the young woman walked over to an old hay wagon, and I saw Mom sign some papers. I was so happy I couldn't stop smiling! After about half an hour, we went home.

Mom told my dad when we got home and he said, "Well, looks like we need to have someone to build us a fence!"

12

Chapter 2:
Samson Is Born!

After a few weeks of watching people out in our yard building fences for two pastures, the day finally arrived when the two horses were going to be delivered to my house! I was sitting in the kitchen, looking out the window, when I saw the old gray horse trailer come up our long driveway. I threw down my pizza and ran outside. I was told to stay back while they backed the trailer into the fenced pasture. I finally heard the rusty door open, and the white mare raced out with the black mare following close behind. They ran for days! A week or two later, the horses started to calm down and let us pet them. Although they were rescued months ago, they still felt the pain, suffering, and neglect they experienced in the past. I knew then it was my job to let them know that absolutely nothing was going to hurt them here and that it was okay to trust me.

On April 23rd, my mom came to visit me at school. I was scared until I saw the big smile on her face as she said, "Ashley, I have a big surprise for you!"

"What is it?" I asked. She handed me a folded paper. I opened it slowly and read it. I screamed at the top of my lungs! The white mare, we call her "Stephie," gave birth to beautiful foal! The skinny chestnut foal was a BOY! Imagine, a stallion. Mom let me go home and see him. I had watched the Saddle Club on TV, and one of the horses had a foal they named Samson. Somehow, that just stuck with me. Our new foal's name is "Samson." It didn't take Samson two days to start following me around like a little puppy.

Baby Pictures!

Spring 2006

Less than one month old

Chapter 3:
Training Begins

Horses have to be three years old before you can start riding them, because the added weight on them hurts their joints. I spent the first three years of Samson's life talking to him and spending time with him every day. I got up an hour before other kids did and took him carrots and water in the barn. After school, I gave him fresh hay and more water. Sometimes I just cleaned stalls and brushed him.

I gave all my time to Samson. I didn't play softball or do many of the things kids my age did. Samson was not only my friend, but also my best friend in which to confide. We talked for hours about school, friends, and even chores that had to be done, and I liked that just fine. Probably all that time talking and bonding with Samson gave me the confidence and patience to train him to do his best.

Breaking a horse is a long, patient process. When Samson grew older and stronger, I threw towels or rugs over his back and walked him around to get him used to a little weight on his back.

Training, 2008 (Photo by Brittany Upole)

Garrett County Mountain Top: Horse Show 2010

Winter training

23

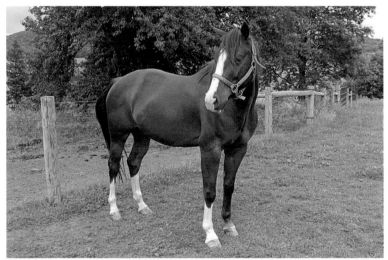

Samson at home, Summer 2011

Ashley with the Maui Horse Whisperer, Maui, Hawaii

Every month that followed brought a new thing Samson had to learn. I put my hands on his back and pushed down like I was going to push myself up on his back. Next, I added a saddle. Then, without the saddle on him, I lay across his back on my belly, hanging my feet off one side and my head and arms off the other side to get him used to my weight.

Finally, the day came when I said, "Okay. We ready for this?" I put the saddle on Samson and put one foot in the stirrup. Okay. Then, I threw my leg over his back and Samson let me sit on him! WOW! We walked around and talked.

I am the only person to have ridden Samson and I'm more proud to ride Samson than any of the registered and professionally trained horses in our stable, because he was born and trained here by me. It means more to me to see Samson win because we were able to rescue his mom and then him.

Once I could ride Samson, I tried to teach him to race around barrels, but instead he jumped the cones. So, I built my own jumps for him to practice in the small ring at my house. I bought fake flowers at the Dollar Store and stuck them in the ground to get him used to jumping over flowers. So, he was learning to be a jumper!

My parents took me to Hawaii on vacation and while we were there, they arranged for me to take lessons from a "horse whisperer." She taught me how to spend time sitting on a horse and to breathe deeply, and breathe out when he breathes in. What a wonderful experience! I couldn't wait to get home to try it on Samson. Little did I know it would be sooner than later at the State Fair!

Chapter 4:
The State Fair

It started as soon as we settled Samson in his stall at the State Fair horse barns.

"What kind is he?" a passerby asked.

"His mother is a paint," I replied.

"He doesn't look like a paint. He looks like a quarter horse. What's he registered as?"

My face burns, but I don't say anything or reply.

"Oh, so he's a mutt!" the man said, shaking his head like he's thinking, Girl, this ain't no 4-H show, and he moves on to the horse in the next stall. I breathe deeply.

I get mad when people call Samson a junk horse and say he can't do it, or that he doesn't have a chance because he's not from a top purebred. I wanted to take him to youth nationals because I know he can compete ...and win. At least give him a chance!

I've competed at the national level; I have nothing to prove—but Samson does. He doesn't have fancy bloodlines and he's not professionally trained. I trained him and I'm fourteen-years-old. I know Samson can do it.

< West Virginia State Fair—Over Fences (Photo by Connor Photography)

Now we are tied for Grand Champion Over Fences at the West Virginia State Fair.

To break the tie, Destiny and I will have to ride our horse to a cone and stop, and then make them turn 360 degrees on their hindquarters. Jumpers are not good doing this!

Neither team did it very prettily, but the judges decided Samson and I are the winners!

My mom said later she thinks the judges could see that I could fix any problem Samson had in the ring and that I really knew my horse.

Of course I do. He's my best friend and I love him more than anything in the world!

The End

Membership Associations

AQHA (American Quarter Horse Association) *www.aqha.com*

APHA (American Paint Horse Association) *www.apha.com*

IEA (Interscholastic Equestrian Association) *www.rideiea.com*

4-H (Youth Development Organization) *www.4-h.org*

FFA (Future Farmers of America Association) *www.ffa.org*

Preston County Livestock Association

Mountaineer Hunter Jumper Association *www.mhja.us*

North Western West Virginia Quarter Horse Association *www.nwvqha.com*

West Virginia Equine Association *www.wvequineassoc.org*

USEF (United States Equine Federation) *www.usef.org*

National Snaffle Bit Association *ww.nsba.com*

American Youth Horse Council *www.ayhc.com*

North American League *www.ryegate.com*

Central Pennsylvania Horseman's Association *www.gotoahorseshow.com*

American Quarter Pony Association *www.aqpa.com*

Welsh Pony & Cob Society of America *www.welshpony.org*

Ohio Quarter Horse Association *www.oqha.com*

National Chincoteague Pony Association *www.pony-chincoteague.com*

Mt Top Saddle Club West Virginia Farm Bureau *www.wvfarm.org*

Teams

Ridge Riders Show Team coached by Michele Koury
www.valleyridgefarm.net

NYATT (National Youth Activity Team Tournament)
www.aqha.com

KDS Show Team coached by Kristina Dulashaw-Swank
www.kdshorses.com

Additionally, Ashley is a member of the American Quarter Horse Association and the National Snaffle Bit Association. Ashley competed with her Quarter Horse, Jamaican Me Skip in several all around events in 2010. Her strongest classes are judged on her skills as a rider. She excels in hunt seat equitation, horsemanship and showmanship. Furthermore, Ashley was awarded the Justin Rookie of the Year Award by the American Quarter Horse Association for accumulating the most all around points by any rookie in West Virginia.

She continued her show career by competing at the 2010 All American Quarter Horse Congress in Ohio. She placed in the top 10 at Congress with Stardom XL in Hunter Hack (2010). As a member of the Northern West Virginia Quarter Horse Association, she accumulated enough points to become a member of the National Youth Activity Team Tournament and she will be representing West Virginia at Congress in the Hunter Under Saddle class and 2011 in Horsemanship.

West Virginia State Fair Ribbons and Champion Trophies

May, 2011, Samson and I achieved our goal of going to Nationals and we placed 3rd in Jumping (Photo by Jeff Kubride Photography)